Solomon's Porch

A WEALTH OF TREASURED WISDOM

an exhortation of proverbs and parables

Solomon's Porch

A Wealth of Treasured Wisdom

an exhortation of proverbs and parables

Complied By
Ophelia S. Lewis

VILLAGE TALES PUBLISHING
U.S.A.

A catalog record for this book is available from the Library of Congress:

LCCN: 2017900123
ISBN: 9781945408106
eISBN: 9781945408113

Published By:
Village Tales Publishing
Lawrenceville, GA

Cover Design By:
OASS

www.villagetalespublishing.com
www.oass.villagetalespublishing.com

Printed in the United States of America

DEDICATION

"Grandmas hold our tiny hands
for just a little while, but our hearts forever."

I dedicate this book to a phenomenal woman,
my dearest grandmother,
Mary Louis Yeke Thorpe

ACKNOWLEDGEMENT

All praise is due to the Creator, God, most high! In God's hand is the life of every living thing; having neither beginning of days, nor end of life, without father, without mother, the only true God.

This journey would not be possible without the support of my family, thanks for always cheering.

My love for parables and provers began with my grandmother. Grandmothers are special people; every time they are around, love pops up. My grandmother was an extraordinary woman, the original 'Yeke Gurl'. Like her, my mother, sisters, and I are 'strong' women. In the sense of being independent women, nasty women, Yeke-girls. Our daughters and granddaughters are the same.

She called every stranger she met, Good-friend; male or female. Everybody called her, Ma Mai, including her grandchildren. Her children called her, Mama. If Ma Mai didn't know you, or your name, she would call you, Good-friend.

So, Ma Mai never was one of those grandmothers who 'spoiled' their grandchildren. She disciplined with tough love. When you got out of control, she'd use a parable or a proverb for scolding. However, everyone knew who her favorite grandchildren were. I was a favorite; she gave me my nickname, Mocco. She loved everybody, though.

What I remembered most about her is, her love for parables and proverbs. The two she used often were; "Looking for work and praying not to find it" and "You do good, you do good for yourself."

Thus, my love for parables and proverbs. We use them with our children even during everyday conversations.

INTRODUCTION

From the almost inexhaustible placer of life, I have been able to retrieve these nuggets; spiritual and cultural. One reason for this book is to introduce this unique collection of parables and proverbs, and enlighten my readers with the stimulating effect I have discovered personally. These nuggets are of intellectual value at best.

The nuggets have been chosen from various cultures and this collection contains the cream of parables which are used all over the world. Many more such nuggets await the discovery of future miners.

CONTENT

A

ABSENCE

❀ He who is absent is always in the wrong.

❀ What the eye doesn't see, the heart doesn't grieve over.

❀ To leave, is to die a little.

❀ He who excuses, accuses himself.

ANGER

❀ Hard words break bones.

ASPIRATION

❀ A man should go on living; if only to satisfy his curiosity.

❀ Against change of fortune, set a brave heart.

❀ Between the wish and the thing, life lay waiting.

❀ Hope is the dream of a soul awake.

❀ No matter how far you have gone on a wrong road, turn back.

❀ The burden one likes is cheerfully carried.

❀ The 'wish' is father to the 'thought'.

❀ When the 'will' is ready, the feet are light.

❀ He who does not look ahead, always remains behind.

❀ Count not what is lost, but what is left.

❀ Great souls have wills; feeble ones have only wishes. [**Chinese**]

AUTHORITY

❀ Every law has its own law.

❀ Fire is a good servant, but a bad master.

❀ A cockroach knows how to sing and dance, but it is the hen that prevents it from performing its art during the day. [**Nigeria**]

❀ A man who uses force is afraid of reasoning. [**Kenya**]

❀ Great towns grow with peace, not by killing or intimidation.

B

BEAUTY

❀ Beauty is not sold and eaten.

❀ Beauty is the wisdom of women; wisdom is the beauty of men.

❀ Beauty passes; wisdom remains.

❀ Charm is better than beauty.

❀ Different flowers look good to different people.

❀ Beauty is the gift of God.

C

CHARACTER

❀ The devil's children have the devil's luck.

❀ A good thing sells itself, a bad one advertises itself.

❀ A man who pays respect to the great, paves the

way for his own greatness.

❀ An okra tree does not grow taller than its master. [Sierra Leone] (*Biblical wisdom suggests "No servant is greater than his master"*)

❀ Don't expect water not to be wet.

❀ A young bamboo cannot be eagerly desired for building [Zambia]

❀ As the dog said, 'If I fall down for you, and you fall down for me, it is playing'.

❀ Better a curtain hanging motionless, than a flag blowing in the wind. [East African]

❀ When you know who his friend is, you know who he is.

❀ To cure a bad sore, you must use bad medicine. [Liberia]

❀ Where you will sit when you are old, shows where you stood in youth.

❀ Wherever man goes to dwell, his character goes with him.

❀ If a child washes his hands, he could eat with kings.

❀ If an arrow has not entered deeply, then its removal is not hard. [Ghana]

❀ Looking at a king's mouth, one would never think he sucked his mother's breast.

❀ No matter how long a log stays in the water, it doesn't become a crocodile. [Mali] (*No matter how much time you spend around others, you can never become them)*

❃ One who bathes willingly with cold water does not feel the cold. [**Tanzania**]

❃ Those whose palm-kernels were cracked for them by another, should not forget to be humble.

❃ You can tell a ripe corn by its looks.

❃ Judge a man by the work of his hands.

❃ A chick that will grow into a cock can be spotted the very day it hatches.

❃ A child's fingers are never scalded by a piece of hot yam which his mother puts into his palm.

❃ A thorn in your foot is temporarily appeased, but it is still in. [**Tanzania**] (*negative impression registered in the brain can produce problem one day*)

❃ Cows are born with ears; later they grow horns. [**Sudanese**]

❃ One who relates with a corrupt person likewise gets corrupted. [**Kenya**]

❃ The eye that you treat is the one that turns against you. [**Kenya**]

❃ One who eats, has tasted the hardship of labor. [**Democratic Republic of Congo**]

❃ The person who tends to ingratiate himself to his father without involving others, never inherits the father's property. [*Kenya*]

❃ A wart hog eating its fill does not delight a pig. [**Mozambique**]

❀ A debt is not a loss, once one know the debtor. [**Democratic Republic of Congo**]

❀ Suffering is prior to attaining success or perfection. [**Tanzania**]

❀ The chief's son has to collect firewood when destiny destroys him. [**Sudanese**]

❀ When you sort out the grains, it becomes pure. [**Ethiopian**]

❀ If you provoke a rattlesnake, prepare to get bitten by it. [**Kenya**]

❀ The thing that will hurt you will always keep on coming back, even if you try to avoid it. [**Tanzania**]

❀ It is not the cook's fault when the cassava turns out to be hard and tasteless. [**Ghana**]

❀ A tree is known by its fruit. [**South African**]

❀ Great fires erupt from tiny sparks. [**Libya**]

❀ A child of the kwale bird (*which hatches its nestling on the ground*) learns to fly. [**Zambia**]

❀ A chicken that keeps scratching the dung-hill will soon find the mother's thigh bones. [**Nigeria**]

❀ When a leaf falls to the ground, the tree gets the blame [**Zambia**]

❀ The hunger that has hope for its satisfaction does not kill. [**Nigeria**]

❀ Alive, we live in the same house or under the same roof. Dead, we rest in the same tomb.

[Madagascar]

* A thieving dog knows itself. [Kenya]

* A deaf ear is followed by death, and an ear that listens is followed by blessings. [Kenya]

* It is only a male elephant that can save another one from a pit. [Democratic Republic of Congo]

* A stick is straightened while still young [Uganda]

* A comb becomes bad when it hurts you.

* Better die with honor than live with shame.

* Gold's father is dirt, yet it regards itself as noble.

* There are two perfectly good men; one dead, and the other unborn. [Chinese]

* Where vice (evil) is, vengeance follows.

* Appearances are deceptive.

* A soft answer turns away wrath.

* One is rated by others as he rates himself.

* The teeth of a man serve as a fence. [Senegalese]

* A donkey knows no gratitude.

* Lying and stealing are next door neighbors.

* Examine what is said, not him who speaks.

* He that flatters you more than you desire, either has deceived you or wishes to deceive.

[Italian]

❀ Whoever gossips to you will gossip about you.

❀ From our ancestors come our names, from our virtues our honors.

❀ A dog that steals sells its body. [Kenya]

❀ One joy scatters a hundred grief. [Chinese]

❀ People know each other better on a journey.

❀ The chicken is never declared in the court of hawks. [Ghana]

❀ Many licks before they bite.

❀ The cat would eat fish, but would not wet her feet.

❀ The good looks of a moron do not stay that way for long. [Ethiopian]

❀ A jack of both sides, is before long, trusted by nobody, and abused by both parties.

❀ An old broom knows the dirty corners best. [Irish]

❀ Familiarity breeds contempt.

❀ In a broken nest there are few whole eggs. [Chinese]

❀ A champion bull starts from birth. [Kenya]

❀ Bad dancing does not break an engagement. [Kenya]

❀ To speak kindly does not hurt the tongue.

* "They say" is often a great liar.

* A clear conscience is a soft pillow.

* A crime eats its own child.

* A good companion shortens the longest road.

* A poor joke must invent its own laughter.

* A worthy man is still worthy even penniless; a donkey is a donkey even if he is finely saddled.

* Gossiping and lying go hand in hand.

* He that does not bring up his son to some honest calling and employment, brings him up to be a thief. [Jewish]

* He, who does evil to others, does it to himself.

* How can you expect to find ivory in a dog's mouth?

* If your buttocks burn, you know you have done wrong.

* It is better to trust the eyes rather than the ears.

* Know thyself.

* Locks keep out only the honest. [Jewish]

* Not everything which is bad comes to hurt us.

* Our faults irritate us most when we see them in others.

* People count the faults of those who keep them waiting.

* Roses fall, but the thorns remain.

* The most beautiful things in the universe are the starry heavens above us and the feeling of duty within us.

* There is nothing noble in being superior to another person. The true nobility is in being superior to your precious self.

* Thorns and roses grow on the same tree.

* To talk goodness is not good...only to do it is. [Chinese]

* What makes us discontented with our condition is the absurdly exaggerated idea we have to the happiness of others.

* When money speaks, the truth is silent.

* You cannot get lost on a straight road.

* When you go to buy, use your eyes not your ears.

* Regular feet cannot be affected by irregular shoes. [Chinese]

* Without grace, beauty is an unabated hook.

* Do not choose your wife at a dance, but in the field among the harvesters.

* All people are your relatives; therefore expect only trouble from them.

* Come live with me and you will know me.

* Fear only two; God and the man who has no fear of God.

❁ A hundred wagon loads of thoughts will not pay a single ounce of debt.

❁ All mankind is divided into three classes: those that are immovable, those that are movable and those that move.

❁ Gifts make their way through stone walls.

❁ When you meet a man, you judge him by his cloths; when you leave, you judge him by his heart.

❁ The man who dictates separates himself from others. [Somalia]

❁ A poor beauty finds more lovers than husbands.

❁ Habits are cobwebs at first; cables at last.

❁ The enemy of my enemy is my friend.

❁ Dogs do not actually prefer bones to meat; it is just that no one ever gives them meat.

❁ He that falls by himself never cries.

❁ Pick up a sesame seed, but lose sight of a watermelon. [Chinese]

❁ If you have never done anything evil, you should not be worrying about devils to knock at your door. [Chinese]

❁ If you stand straight, do not fear a crooked shadow. [Chinese]

❁ Conscience makes cowards of us all.

❁ Vicious as a tigress can be, she never eats her

own cubs. [**Chinese**]

❀ When a fox preaches, take care of your geese.

❀ Give and take is fair play.

❀ I know by my own pot how the others boil.

❀ If a job's worth doing, it's worth doing well.

❀ A family name is not cooked and eaten, one's life is the thing.

❀ A good name is better than gold.

❀ A performing masquerade who tries too hard to outclass his colleagues may expose his anus.

❀ He who is courteous is not a fool.

❀ It is from a small seed that the giant iroko tree has its beginning.

❀ Man counts what he has refused, not what he has given.

❀ If a child is not well-behaved, she is not sent by the mother to go alone to the market to buy things for her.

❀ If gold rusts, what will iron do?

❀ Eat less; taste more.

❀ If there is a strong general, there will be no weak soldiers.

❀ It does not matter if the cat is black or white, so long it catches mice.

❀ It is for saying that he has no time that the

monkey's body became over-grown with long hairs.

* It is the fortunate person that the physician undertakes to help.

* Self-love of the king parrot that made him become a talkative.

* It is usual of a person found guilty in a trial to boast that he would press his case further.

* It is what the eyes of one man sees that is described as a boa constrictor.

* Get a thief to catch a thief.

* The one chased away with a club comes back; but the one chased away with reason does not. [Kenya]

* A little body often harbors a great soul.

* Reshape one's foot to try to fit into a new shoe.

* Respect starts with yourself.

* Ease and honor are seldom bedfellows.

* Empty sacks will never stand upright.

* No one is worse for knowing the worst of themselves.

* A maker of idols is never an idolater.

* A razor may be sharper than an ax, but it cannot cut wood.

* An eagle does not catch flies.

* Bad things never walk alone. [**Chinese**]

* Beauty, unaccompanied by virtue, is as a flower without perfume.

* Before the chicken, carefully observe the character of your guest. [**Mandingo**]

* Change the skin, wash the heart.

* Diamond cuts diamond.

* If you put a silk dress on a goat, he is a goat still.

* It is very hard to shave an egg.

* The whisper of a pretty girl can be heard further than the roar of a lion.

* What is in the marrow is hard to take out of the bone.

* Wherever man goes to dwell, his character goes with him.

* One person in a street kills a dog, and the street is named a street of dog killers.

* The man who is honored, has first honored himself.

* When a woman cannot have good palm-nuts to give her rich oil, she still has to maintain decency in order to remain one of those that sell good quality oil.

* The wolf changes his coat, but not his disposition.

* Love and cough cannot be hid.

❧ Good men must die, but death cannot kill their names.

❧ A bottle of oil warmed over the fire has no means of producing oil by itself.

❧ If one imitates the upright, one becomes upright; if one imitates the crooked, one becomes crooked.

❧ Even an old woman may run when a goat carries her snuff-box.

❧ When a ripe fruit sees an honest man, it drops.

❧ Washing with dirty water does not clean a dirty object. [**Liberia**]

❧ If one imitates the upright, one becomes upright; if one imitates the crook, one becomes crooked.

COMMON-SENSE

❧ Hunger is a good cook.

❧ Study from new books, but from old teachers.

❧ By bravely enduring it, an evil which cannot be avoided is overcome.

❧ Don't cry before you're hurt.

❧ Good habits result from resisting temptation.

❧ Kind words are worth much and they cost little.

❧ Pay beforehand was never well served.

❈ When in doubt, do not.

❈ You can drive out nature with a pitchfork, but she keeps on coming back.

❈ He travels fastest who travels alone.

❈ Self-praise is no recommendation.

❈ A fish is the last to acknowledge the existence of water.

❈ A man who is trampled to death by an elephant is a man who is blind and deaf.

❈ A hunter who has only one arrow does not shoot with careless aim.

❈ A mouse that removes the palm-nut that turns out to be the bait of a trap, would already have known that the palm-nut does not ripen on the ground.

❈ One cannot go back to the farmer from whom one borrowed seed-yams to plant to say that the beetles have eaten up the seed-yams.

❈ If one were to remove every smoking wood from a fire and condemn it as bad, one would be killing the fire itself.

❈ It takes wisdom to prevent someone from whom one cannot accept repayment to have access to one's valuable possessions.

❈ It is the brutally outspoken man that earns enmity

❈ The elephant and the tiger do not go hunting on the same pasture.

* A farmer does not boast that he has had a good harvest until his stock of yams lasts till the following harvest season.

* He who pursues an innocent chicken always stumbles.

* The fish that can see that its water is getting shallower, cannot be stranded.

* Without knowing a way thoroughly at day time, never attempt to pass it at night.

* It is only the tortoise that moves and carries its shell about, which it calls its house.

* It is not enough to run, one must arrive and know when one has arrived.

* A man who lives on the bank of a river does not use spittle to wash his hands.

* We do not use our bare feet to search for hidden thorns which we have seen in day time.

* When will the goat be strong enough to kill a leopard?

* Every river knows where its water would not be soaked up into the earth, and that is where it flows past.

* Common sense hides shame.

* If you climb up a tree, you must climb down the same tree.

* Follow love and it will flee; flee love and it will follow.

* If the owner of a calabash calls it a worthless

calabash, others will join him to use it to pack rubbish.

❀ Milk the cow, but do not pull off the udder.

❀ A good meal ought to begin with hunger.

❀ Caution is the parent of safety.

❀ Do not climb a tree to look for a fish.

❀ He who does not have common sense at age thirty will never have it.

❀ In bad fortune, hold out; in good, hold in.

❀ One does not burn a blanket to get rid of a flea.

❀ Part with your head, but not with your secret.

❀ Please your eyes and curse your heart.

❀ Steal a bell with one's ears covered.

❀ Thought is free.

❀ To climb a tree to catch a fish is talking much and doing nothing.

❀ Why keep a dog and bark yourself?

COMMUNICATE

❀ One dog barks at something, the rest bark at him. [Chinese]

❀ Silence means consent.

❀ Harsh words and poor reasoning never settle anything.

❀ Never tell your story to a deaf man.

❀ Don't tell your complaint to one who has no pity.

CONFIDENCE

❀ A good swordsman is not given to quarrel.

❀ A masquerade does not perform to an outside audience until he performs well at the home base.

❀ A masquerade is not a spirit; only because of its mask.

❀ A reed before the wind lives on, while mighty oaks do fall.

❀ Better to bend in the wind than to break.

❀ No wind is of service to him that is bound for nowhere.

❀ The greatest conqueror is he who overcomes the enemy without a blow.

❀ Whoever does not respect confidence will never find happiness in their path.

CONSEQUENCES

❀ A good thing sells itself, a bad one advertises itself.

❀ A man who is advised and he takes it, is still a man who acts from his own free will.

* A single beam cannot support a great house.

* Do not kill the hen for her eggs.

* He, who digs a pit for others, must invariably fall into it.

* If hunger forces a farmer in a particular year to eat both his yam tubers and the seed-yams, the succeeding years would still be worse because he would have no yams to eat and none to plant.

* It is the fear of what tomorrow may bring that makes the tortoise to carry his house along with him wherever he goes.

* Sometimes the rain might force a man more than once to seek shelter under the same tree.

* When the roots of a tree begin to decay, it spreads death to the branches.

* When your mouth stumbles, it's worse than feet.

* Evil enters like needle and spreads like an oak tree. [**Ethiopian**]

* Merit is often an obstacle to fortune; the reason is, it produces two bad effects, envy and fear.

* Offenders never pardon.

* While we pursue happiness, we flee from contentment.

* We pay when old, for the excesses of youth.

CONTENTMENT

* Go further and pay for worst.

* The glow-works light the nights, but more so, the night that their mother prepares porridge.

* When all you have is a hammer, everything looks like a nail.

COOPERATION

* Enough shovels of earth, a mountain; enough pails of water, a river. [Chinese]

* Man is the head of the family; woman the neck that turns the head.

* Many hands make light work. [Tanzania]

* How easy it is to defeat people who do not kindle fire for themselves. [Kenya] *kindling the fire means people coming together and discussing issues. Where there is no unity, people will have no love or value for one another. In Africa, people sit around the fire to discuss issues and to solve conflicts in order to bring peace and unity to their community.*

* The old woman looks after the child to grow its teeth and the young one in turn, looks after the old woman when she loses her teeth. [Ghana]

* When you are at home, your troubles can never defeat you. [Ghana]

* An herbalist that refuses to ask laymen what

leaves he looks for in the bush, must have difficulties getting what he wants.

❀ A housewife who complains that there is not
enough foodstuff in the market should remember that if her husband adds to what is already
available, there would be more for everyone.

❀ A man cannot sit down alone to plan for prosperity.

❀ A man who lives alone is either always over-
worked, or always overfed.

❀ A man who walks alone carries a load of palm-
fronds.

❀ One man cannot build a house.

❀ A single tree cannot make a forest.

❀ If a child shoots an arrow that reaches the top
of a tall palm tree, then it must be that an elderly
person carved the arrow for him.

❀ If a drum is not made, it is the fault of the master; but if the drum is made and is not beaten,
then that is the fault of the boys.

❀ If one would not eat pounded yam for its own
sake, one can still eat it for the sake of the soup
that goes with it. [**Nigeria**]

❀ Two men in a burning house must not stop to
argue.

❀ When an elephant falls, meat is sure to be surplus for those who follow the hunter.

❀ When the right hand washes the left hand and

the left hand washes the right hand, both hands become clean.

* When the teeth fall off, the nose is sure to collapse.

* Where water is boss, the land must obey.

* A rich person does not have to struggle, share the problems of ordinary people. [**Tanzania**] (*remain poor in spirit despite your high position*)

* When a blind man carries a lame man, both go forward.

* Only when all contribute their firewood, can they build up a strong fire. [**Chinese**]

* When spider webs unite, they can tie up a lion. [**Ethiopian**]

* Contraries are cured by contraries.

* If the young knew and the old could, there is nothing that couldn't be done.

* There is safety in numbers.

COURAGE

* If you fear something, you give it power over you.

* One who enters the forest does not listen to the breaking of the twigs in the brush. [**Zambia**] (*One who embarks upon a task should not begin to fear or look for the slightest obstacles in his or her endeavours*)

❁ When a needle falls into a deep well, many people will look into the well, but few will be ready to go down after it.

❁ When there is no enemy within, the enemies outside cannot hurt you.

❁ When the moon is shining the cripple becomes hungry for a walk.

❁ Nothing is impossible to a willing heart.

❁ A bully is always a coward.

❁ A lion sleeps in the heart of every brave man.

❁ Fortune favors the bold, but abandons the timid.

❁ It is better to be a coward for a minute than dead for the rest of your life.

❁ Fear is a great inventor.

❁ Worry gives a small thing a big shadow.

❁ In a flat country a hillock (*mound or small hill*) thinks itself a mountain.

❁ Cowards have dreams, brave men have visions.

❁ One who would pick the roses must bear with the thorns.

❁ Tears are best dried with your own hands.

❁ The eye is a coward. [**Kenya**]

❁ The spirit that keeps one going, when one has no choice of what else to do, must not be mistaken for valor.

* Charms do not perform miracles on the shelf; they perform for those who are brave.

* Courage is the father of success.

* No wind, no waves. [**Chinese**]

* Not the glittering weapon fights the fight, but rather the hero's heart.

* One cannot refuse to eat just because there is a chance of being choked.

* Some have been thought brave because they didn't have the courage to run away.

CRITICISM

* A deaf husband and a blind wife are always a happy couple.

* Blame is a lazy man's wages.

* Every flow has its ebb (*outward flow*).

* Everybody joins to blame or condemn a child who overthrows the pot of soup.

* He that has no children brings them up well.

* If a man would live in peace, he would be blind, deaf, and dumb.

* It is easier to pull down than to build up.

* One story is good till another is told.

* One who sees something good must narrate it. [**Uganda**]

❀ Speak not of my debts unless you mean to pay them

❀ The soldier who retreats fifty paces, jeers at the one who retreats one hundred paces. [Chinese]

❀ Whoever digs a pit for his neighbor should dig it his own size.

❀ Wink at small faults, for you have great ones yourself

❀ He who cannot dance will say, "The drum is bad."

❀ The camel does not see the bend in its neck. [Libya]

❀ The mouth which eats does not talk.

❀ A man who has one finger pointing at another has three pointing towards himself.

❀ Criticism is easy but it does not create.

❀ He who digs a pit for others must invariably fall into it.

❀ If a person who curses another is not better than the person he curses, a request is never made of him to rescind the curse.

❀ When the laborer is praised, his cutlass begins to cut more keenly.

❀ Without knowing a person we must not hate him.

❀ Harsh words and poor reasoning never settle anything.

* Have a mouth as sharp as a dagger, but a heart as soft as fufu.

* Do not tell the man who is carrying you that he stinks.

D

DEATH

* Death always comes too early or too late.

* Death is the shadow that always follows the body.

* Death pays all debts.

* Even rabbits insult a dead lion.

* Heaven has a road, but no one travels it; hell has no gate, but men will dig to get there.

* It is better to sit down than to stand, it is better to lie down than to sit, but death is the best of all.

* Six feet of earth make all equal.

* There is a remedy for everything except death.

* We all end up in a single bed; sooner or later.

* When a dying man cries, it is not because of where he is going, which he knows nothing about; but because of what he wishes he would

have done in the world he is leaving behind.

DEBT

❀ A small debt makes a man your debtor; a large one your enemy.

❀ Better to go to bed hungry than to wake up in debt

❀ Eat and drink with your friends, but do not trade with them.

❀ He that cannot pay let him pray.

❀ He who borrows gets sorrows.

❀ Never spend your money before you have it.

❀ Out of debt, out of danger.

❀ Quick to borrow is always slow to pay.

DESPERATION

❀ A drowning man will clutch at a straw.

❀ At the narrow passage, there is no brother and no friend.

DISCIPLINE

❀ Better a snotty child than his nose wiped off.

❀ A child who has no mother will not have scars to show on his back.

❀ A piece of iron can only become what the blacksmith says it should become.

❀ It is the habit that a child forms at home, that follows them to their marriage.

❀ Rebuke should have a grain more of salt than of sugar.

DISHONESTY

❀ No deception is more dangerous than self-deception.

❀ A liar ought to have a good memory.

❀ When money is taken, freedom is forsaken.

DIVERSITY

❀ Variety is the spice of life.

DOUBTING THOMAS

❀ Forewarned, forearmed.

❀ Skeptics are never deceived.

❀ Believe nothing and be on your guard against everything.

❀ Blind belief is dangerous. [Kenya]

❀ Doubt is the key to knowledge.

❀ Great doubts, deep wisdom; small doubts, little wisdom. [**Chinese**]

E

ENEMIES

* Dangerous enemies will meet again in narrow streets.

* Dead, though the oil-palm may be, the maggot in it lives on.

* There is no little enemy.

* A thousand friends are too few; one enemy is one too many.

* Little enemies and little wounds must not be despised.

EXPERIENCE

* Experience is a comb which nature gives to men when they are bald.

* Experience is the mother of wisdom.

* From the faults of another, a wise man will correct his own.

* He who has been bitten by a snake, fears a

piece of string.

* Only he that has traveled the road knows where the holes are deep.

* The old horse will know the way.

* To understand your parents' love, you must raise children yourself.

* We start as fools and become wise through experience.

* Do not expect old heads upon young shoulders.

* A pad that breaks a pot of water does not remain on the head.

* A fall into a ditch makes you wiser.

* A gem cannot be polished without friction, nor a man perfected without trials. [**Chinese**]

* To know the road ahead, ask those coming back.

* He who has not tasted the bitter does not understand the sweet. [**Chinese**]

* The older the fiddle, the sweeter the tune.

F

FAILURE

❀ The great question is not whether you have failed, but whether you are content with failure. [Chinese]

❀ Failure is the mother of success.

❀ Success has many fathers, while failure is an orphan.

FAITH

❀ Weave in faith and God will find the thread.

❀ There are no miracles for those that have no faith in them.

❀ God will provide – ah, if only He would till He does!

❀ Man's extremity is God's opportunity.

❀ Short prayers reach heaven.

❀ Faith will remove mountains.

❀ Ask God for what man can give, and you may get it.

❀ God's plans always lead to victory.

FAMILY

* A sea refuses no river.

* Children suck the mother when they are young and their father when they are old.

* It takes a whole village to raise a child.

* My son is my son till he gets him a wife; but my daughter is my daughter all the days of her life.

* There is not so much comfort in having children as there is sorrow in parting with them.

* We do not inherit the land from our ancestors; we borrow it from our children.

* A family name is not cooked and eaten; one's life is the thing.

* A person who has children does not die.

* An ounce of blood is worth more than a pound of friendship.

* It is an irresponsible adult that creates enmity because of a disagreement that arises between two children.

* It is he, who has no place to call at, that moves fast through life.

* It is in the shelter of each other that the people live.

* Look for the good, not the evil, in the conduct of members of the family.

* The fly that has no one to advise it, follows the

corpse into the grave.

❀ No frog is tied by a rope to a pond.

❀ We cannot choose who our relatives should be, even though we may come to like some better than others.

❀ When a man loses his prestige, he does not regain it by going to where he is not known.

❀ A man that begets a barren cannot have a grandchild.

❀ One father is more than a hundred schoolmasters.

FLATTERY

❀ Imitation is the sincerest form of flattery.

❀ Lawyers and painters can soon make what's black, white.

❀ There are no greater promisors than those who have nothing to give.

FOOLS

❀ A fool dreams of wealth; a wise man, of happiness.

❀ A fool has many days. [Kenya]

❀ Fools look for dung where the cow never borrowed.

* A wise man changes his mind, a fool never will.

* A wise man remembers his friends at all times; a fool, only when he has need of them.

* Better a wise foe than a foolish friend.

* Don't dance at a volcano.

* Fools and obstinate men make lawyers rich.

* Fools ask questions that wise men cannot answer.

* Fools build houses; wise men buy them.

* He alone is wise who can accommodate himself to all contingencies of life; but the fool contends, and struggling, like a swimmer, against the stream.

* He who asks the question is a fool for a minute; he who does not is a fool forever. [Chinese]

* He who is born a fool is never cured.

* He who undertakes to be his own teacher has a fool for a pupil.

* He, who asks is a fool for five minutes; but he who does not ask remains a fool forever.

* If you run after two hares, you will catch neither.

* Insanity is doing the same thing in the same way and expecting a different outcome. [Chinese]

* It is a wise man that lives with money in the bank; it is a fool who dies that way.

❀ It is foolhardy to climb two trees at once just because one has two feet. [Ethiopian]

❀ Many talk like philosophers, yet live like fools

❀ Money has the capability of making people laugh; but when they laugh, the foolish ones sometimes forget to close their mouths.

❀ One never needs their humor as much as when they argue with a fool.

❀ Reason is the wise man's guide; example the fool's.

❀ The foolish cannot be leaders. [Kenya]

❀ Only a fool tests the depth of the water with both feet.

❀ The wise continues while the fool is always beginning. [Zambia]

❀ There's no fool like an old fool.

❀ What the fool does in the end, the wise do in the beginning.

❀ When a fool is cursed, he thinks he is being praised.

❀ When the blind man bears the standard, pity those who follow.

❀ Young people talk of what they are doing; old people of what they have done; and fools of what they have a mind to do.

❀ A fool is like a wanderer lost on a path. [Luo]

❀ The fool speaks, the wise man listens. [Ethiopian]

❀ Everybody loves a fool, but nobody wants him for a son. [Ivorian]

❀ He is a fool whose sheep runs away twice. [Ghana]

FORGIVENESS

❀ Forgive and forget.

❀ Never repeat old grievances.

❀ Pardon is the choicest flower of victory.

❀ Revenge converts a little right into a great wrong.

❀ The noblest vengeance is to forgive.

❀ Write kindness in marble, and write injuries in the dust.

FRIENDSHIP

❀ A reconciled friend is a double enemy.

❀ Be slow in choosing a friend, but slower in changing him.

❀ Broken friendships can be soldered, but never sound.

❀ A friend is known when needed.

❀ A friend is someone who doesn't like the same people you do.

❀ A good friend shields you from the storm.

❀ A man should choose a friend who is better than himself.

❀ Ceremony is the smoke of friendship.

❀ Do not protect yourself by a fence, but rather by your friends.

❀ Hold a true friend with both hands. [**Nigeria**]

❀ If there is cause to someone, the cause to love has just begun.

❀ It is in the shelter of each other that the people live.

❀ It is prosperity that gives us friends; adversity that proves them.

❀ Only your real friends will tell you when your face is dirty.

❀ Over a long distance, you learn about the strength of your horse; over a long time, you learn about the character of your friend.

❀ Rather than tell a lie to help a friend, it is better to assist him in paying the fine for his offense.

❀ Return to old watering holes for more than water; friends and dreams are there to meet you.

❀ Sorrow is like a precious treasure, shown only to friends.

❀ Tell me who's your friend, and I'll tell you who you are.

❀ Tell your friend a lie; if he keeps it secret, then

tell him the truth.

* The best mirror is an old friend.

* The road to a friend's house is never long.

* There is something in the misfortune of our best friends which does not displease us.

* To eat from the same pot with another man, is to take an oath of perpetual friendship with him.

* Your friend has a friend; don't tell him.

* False friends are worst than bitter enemies.

* Hedges between keep friendships green.

* Once a friend, always a friend.

* Short reckonings make long friends.

* The time to make friends is before you need them.

* With true friends, even water drunk together is sweet enough. [Chinese]

G

GENEROSITY & SHARING

* Gifts dissolve rocks.

❀ It is an unthinking man who achieves prosperity, and then finds with time, that his body can no longer pass through the door.

❀ The bird that remembers its flockmates never missed the way.

❀ The head could not have gotten to where it is now if it did not give.

❀ The hyena with a cup does not eat up all the available food. [**Kenya**] (*people with basically very little to eat nevertheless share with others who have even less.*)

❀ The man who remembers others, remembers also his creator.

❀ The saving man becomes the free man. [**Chinese**]

❀ To advise is easier than to help.

GOD

❀ God is the true judge of the heart.

❀ Man does what he can; God does what He will.

❀ "Take what you want," God said to man, "and pay for it."

❀ If God breaks your leg, He will teach you how to limp. [**Ghana**]

❀ When your enemy digs a grave for you, God gives you an emergency exit. [**Burundi**]

❀ When God cooks, you don't see smoke. [**Zambia]

* God is closest to those with broken hearts.

* Mankind fears an evil man, but heaven does not.

* When man speaks of the future, God laughs.

* When God punishes a land, He deprives its leaders of wisdom.

* Work is our business; success is God's.

* God made the country and man made the town.

* God sends meat, but the Devil sends cooks.

* Man proposes and God disposes.

* Who God does not teach, man cannot.

* God is a great eye; He sees everything in the world – [Sudanese]

* Life without God is like an un-sharpened pencil; it has no point.

GOOD BEHAVIOR

* A child is what you put into him.

* A child who fears beating would never admit that he played with a missing knife.

* A child's face is his mirror.

* A good name is better than gold.

❀ A man, who eases himself in public, gives cause to others to despise him.

❀ A man who is advised and he takes it, is still a man who acts from his own free will.

❀ Greatness and beauty do not belong to the gods alone.

❀ He who is called a man must behave like a man.

❀ When a face is sullen, it remains there to be seen on its owner.

❀ When a fowl gets to a new town, it stands on one leg until it knows that it is a town where people stand on their two legs.

GOSSIP

❀ Go abroad and you'll hear news from home.

❀ If you can't get people to listen to you any other way, tell them it's confidential.

❀ Little leaks sink the ship.

❀ What is told in the ear of a man is often heard a hundred miles away.

❀ Whoever speaks evil to you of others will speak evil of you to others.

❀ Gossiping and lying go hand in hand.

GRATITUDE

❀ A person on whose head lice are being removed, must be grateful.

❀ By being grateful, a man makes himself deserving of yet another kindness.

GREED

❀ Gambling is the son of greed and the father of despair.

❀ A chicken eats corn, drinks water and swallows little pebbles, but still complains of having no teeth. If she had teeth, would she eat steel? [Nigeria]

❀ Don't lose the four that you already have while running after the eight. [Kenya]

❀ Glutton; one who digs his grave with his teeth.

❀ If you run after two hares you will catch neither.

❀ He that eats till he is sick must fast till he is well.

❀ Many have too much, but none enough.

❀ A bag that says it will not take more and a traditional doctor who says he would not leave anything behind are both sure to suffer.

❀ A man with too much ambition cannot sleep in peace.

❀ A stranger has big eyes, but sees nothing.

❀ A strong man is remembered on the day of the fight and gluttony, on the day food is surplus.

❀ He, whose throat is longer than his arm, must pray constantly for God's protection.

❀ If one eats less, one will taste more.

❀ One can only try to get what one can from the head of an elephant; no one ever carries it home.

❀ One cannot both feast and become rich. [Ghana]

❀ The alcohol that is insufficient for a whole town ought not to intoxicate one man.

❀ The leech that does not let go, even when it is full, dies on the dry land.

❀ Those who are carrying elephants home on their heads need not use their toes to dig up crickets on the way.

❀ More than we use is more than we want.

❀ Appetite comes with eating; the more one has, the more one would have.

❀ If one is roasting two cassavas, one of them is bound to get charred. [Kenya]

❀ The rich are always complaining.

❀ If a greedy eater is near a patient, such a patient can never survive.

❀ A neighbor's hen looks as big as a goose, and his wife as young as a girl.

❀ Stretch your feet according to your blanket.

❀ The leaf that is very sweet in a goat's mouth sometimes hurts his stomach. [**Liberia**]

GUESTS

❀ Every guest hated the others, and the host hated them all.

❀ Let the guest come so that the host may benefit. (feel well) [**Eastern and Central Africa**] (*the arrival of a guest meant a big meal of welcome, perhaps killing a chicken or a goat; also, the guest may be bringing good news or even gifts*)

❀ Fresh fish and new-come guests smell when they are three days old.

❀ He who comes from afar may lie without fear of contradiction as he is sure to be listened to with the utmost attention.

❀ Visits always give pleasure; if not the arrival, the departure.

GUILT

❀ When a person regrets endlessly, he gets to pay more for what he regrets

❀ A guilty conscience needs no accuser

H

HAPPINESS

❀ Call no man happy till he dies.

❀ Happiness is like a sunbeam which the least shadow intercepts, while adversity is often as the rain of spring. [Chinese]

❀ Happy is the country that has no history

❀ If you want happiness for an hour, take a nap; if you want happiness for a day, go fishing; if you want happiness for a month, get married; if you want happiness for a year, inherit a fortune; if you want happiness for a lifetime, help someone else. [Chinese]

❀ Seeking happiness is the straight way to misery.

❀ When a heart is on fire, sparks always fly out of the mouth.

❀ When ambition ends, happiness begins. [Hungarian]

❀ Being happy is better than being king.

❀ To be happy in one's home is better than to be a chief. [Nigeria]

❀ Where one is wise two are happy.

HARD WORK

* A farmer does not conclude by the mere look of it that a corn is unripe; he tears it open for examination.

* A farmer, who would not work inside the rain and would not work under the sun, would have nothing to harvest at the end of the farming year

* A single beam cannot support a great house.

* An ant-hill that is destined to become a giant ant-hill will definitely become one, no matter how many times it is destroyed by elephants.

* Begin to weave and God will give the thread.

* Climb mountains to see lowlands. [**Chinese**]

* Do not wait until you're thirsty to dig a well.

* Far is where there is nothing; where something is, you will struggle to the death to reach it [**Zimbabwe**] (*one aiming for the valued goal will expand even to death to reach it*)

* Footprints on the sands of time are not made by sitting down.

* God gives the nuts, but He does not crack them.

* It does not matter if the cat is black or white, as long as it catches mice.

* It is the work of one's hands that decides what one eats for dinner; for some it is pounded yam, for others it is pounded plantain or nothing.

❀ No bees, no honey; no work, no money.

❀ Only time and effort brings proficiency.

❀ Sow melon, reap melon; sow beans, reap beans.

❀ Sow much, reap much; sow little, reap little. [Chinese]

❀ Success is 10% ability, and 90% sweat.

❀ Talk doesn't cook rice.

❀ The heap of yams you will reap, depends upon the number of mounds you have plowed.

❀ The journey is the reward. [Chinese]

❀ The lizard that jumped from the high iroko tree to the ground said he would praise himself if no one else did.

❀ The path is made by walking.

❀ The wasp says that several regular trips to a mud pit enable it to build a house.[Ghana] (*persistence yields results*)

❀ To do one's duty is to eat the prized fruit of honor.

❀ To open a shop is easy; to keep it open is an art.

❀ Tomorrow belongs to the people who prepare for it today.

❀ We live by hope, but a reed never becomes an iroko tree by dreaming.

❀ When a needle falls into a deep well, many people will look into the well, but few will be ready to do down after it.

* Work expands so as to fill the time available.

* Work relieves us from three great evils; boredom, vice and want.

* You must crack the nuts before you can eat the kernel.

* Teachers open the door, but you must enter by yourself.

* If you want a thing done, go; if not, send.

* It is a pot of water that is already half full that the world would like to help in filling to the brim.

* He that will eat the fruit must climb the tree.

* The greatest step is out the door.

HATE

* The ashes fly back into the face of him who throws them.

* He who has done evil expects evil.

* If your mouth turns into a knife, it will cut off your lips.

* It is better to be loved than feared.

* It is the calm and silent water that drowns a man.

* Two birds disputed about a kernel, when a third swooped down and carried it off.

❀ There is no medicine to cure hatred.

❀ The fire you kindle for your enemy often burns yourself more than him.

❀ Who digs a pit for others will fall in.

❀ When pointing an evil finger at a man, three fingers are also pointing at yourself. [Liberia]

HEALTH

❀ A man too busy to take care of his health is like a mechanic too busy to take care of his tools.

❀ A surgeon should be young; a physician, old.

❀ Illness comes by the pound and goes away by the ounce.

❀ As the person who has health is young, so the person who owes nothing is rich.

❀ He who enjoys good health is rich, though he knows it not.

❀ To extend your life by a year, take one less bite each meal.

HONESTY

❀ He who sacrifices his conscience to ambition, burns a picture to obtain the ashes. [Chinese]

❀ Honest advice is unpleasant to the ear.

❀ A person who picks something and decides to

make it his own, ought to think how he would feel if he was the person who lost the property he picked.

❀ Eloquence provides only persuasion, but truth buys loyalty.

❀ Money does not announce how it is earned, but whereas, properly earned money appreciates, improperly earned money depreciates.

❀ Rather than tell a lie to help a friend, it is better to assist him in paying the fine for his offense.

❀ The bottom of wealth is sometimes a dirty thing to behold.

❀ If you would be well served, serve yourself.

❀ The first step toward greatness is to be honest.

❀ Truth fears no trial.

❀ Whoever tells the truth is chased out of nine villages.

❀ The woman who tells her age is either too young to have anything to lose or too old to have anything to gain.

❀ The word of a friend makes you cry; the word of an enemy makes you cry. [**Algeria**] (*advice given by someone who has your best interest at heart is sometimes unpleasant and even painful, but the person who seeks your downfall may deliberately encourage you toward hidden danger with advice that seems pleasant and good*)

❀ Looking for work and praying not to find it.

HOPE

* Wreck on shore is a beacon at sea.

* He who has health, has hope; he who has hope, has everything.

* Hope is the last to abandon the unhappy.

* Sing before breakfast, cry before night.

* The pillar of the world is hope. [Nigeria]

* To the fighting man, peace is sure.

* Hope is a good breakfast, but a bad supper.

* It is better to travel hopefully than to arrive.

* He that lives in hope, dances to an ill tune.

* Were it not for hope, the heart would break.

HUMOR

* Man fools himself; he prays for a long life and he fears old age.

* The child we had yesterday says he will not play with us; before we had him, who did we play with? [Nigeria]

HYPOCRISY

* There is honor among thieves.

* Things are not always what they seem.

* You cannot run with the hare and hunt with the hounds.

* You suffer from smoke produced by the firewood you fetched yourself. [Kenya]

* Don't think that because a goat grinds its teeth there is food in its mouth.

I

IGNORANCE

* A little knowledge is a dangerous thing.

* Beware of one who has nothing to lose.

* Fear an ignorant man more than a lion.

* Ignorance does not kill you, but it makes you sweat a lot.

* Instruction in youth is like engraving in stones.

* Learning is a treasure that will follow its owner everywhere.

* Take heed you do not find what you do not seek.

INTEGRITY

❀ A man trying to sell a blind horse always praises its feet.

❀ Better suffer for the truth than prosper in falsehood.

❀ There is no greater fraud than a promise not kept.

❀ Work as if you were to live forever; live as if you were to die tomorrow.

❀ You cannot drive straight on a twisting lane.

❀ If you have integrity, nothing else matters; if you don't have integrity, nothing else matters.

❀ It's difficult to choose between two blind goats

❀ Sell not virtue to purchase wealth.

❀ With virtue, you cannot be entirely poor; without virtue, you cannot really be rich. [**Chinese**]

❀ Don't set sail on someone else's star.

❀ Good seed makes good crop.

J

JEALOUSY

✿ Envy eats nothing but its own heart.

✿ It is a poor heart that never rejoices.

✿ Rivalry is not good for fowls, and it is not good for goats; worse still, it is not good for human beings.

K

KINDNESS

✿ One joy scatters a hundred grief.

✿ The man who gives little with a smile gives more than the man who gives much with a frown. [Jewish]

✿ A bit of fragrance always clings to the hand that gives you roses.

✿ Do not use a hatchet to remove a fly from your friend's forehead.

❀ Good management is better than good income.

❀ Goodness speaks in a whisper, evil shouts.

❀ If men were now to turn their hostility towards the cat, it would not be long before the domestic cat becomes a wild animal.

❀ If you wish to do a good deed, consult no one.

❀ Kindness begets kindness.

❀ Men never moan over the opportunities lost to do good, only the opportunities to be bad.

❀ That which is good is never finished. [**Tanzania**]

❀ The miser and the open-handed spend the same in the long run.

❀ Those who derive fun watching lunatics, ought to have one as a child or relation to know the pains of it.

❀ When a sickle is drawn, it in turn draws the tree to which it is hooked.

❀ One can pay back the loan of gold, but one dies forever in debt to those who are kind. [**Malayan**]

KNOWLEDGE

❀ A proverb is the child of experience.

❀ Give a man a fish and you feed him for a day; teach a man to fish and you feed him for a lifetime.

❧ If you are planning for a year, sow rice; if you are planning for a decade, plant trees; if you are planning for a lifetime, educate people.

❧ Learning is like the horizon; there is no limit.

❧ When you cease to strive to understand, then you will know without understanding.

❧ Wonders will never cease.

❧ Write down the advice of him who loves you, though you like it not at present.

L

LAW

❧ Hard cases make bad law.

❧ Liberty has no crueler enemy than license.

❧ One hour in the execution of justice is worth seventy years of prayers.

❧ Law helps those who watch, not those who sleep.

❧ The more laws the less justice.

❧ Necessity knows no law.

❧ Where the law is uncertain, there is no law.

❀ Lawyers and woodpeckers have long bills.

LAZINESS

❀ Slow help is no help.

❀ The devil finds work for the idle hands to do.

❀ The devil tempts all men, but idle men tempt the devil.

❀ The man who has nothing to do is always the busiest.

❀ Tomorrow is often the busiest day of the week.

❀ Vision without action is a daydream; action without vision is a nightmare. [Japanese]

❀ A weapon which you don't have in your hand won't kill a snake.

❀ A tree not taller than an ant, cannot shade you. [Nigeria]

❀ He who is afraid of doing too much always does too little.

❀ It is a lazy man who says, "It is only because I have no time that my farm is overgrown with weeds".

❀ It is not work that kills, but worry.

❀ Make sure to send a lazy man the angel of death.

❀ Rest breeds rust.

* Resilient strength and big muscles do not make a farmer.

* Sleep and indolence are not cousins of a good harvest.

* The lazier a man is, the more he plans to do tomorrow.

* Water that has been begged for does not quench the thirst. [Uganda] *In most cases, what is received that is bagged for turns out to be less than what the person needs or desires.*

* You will never plow a field by turning it over in your mind.

* A person who does not cultivate his farm well always says that it has been bewitched. [Tanzania]

* A man grows most tired while standing still.

* A young man idle, an old man needy.

* Be not afraid of going slowly; be afraid only of standing still.

* He that is doing nothing is seldom in need of helpers.

* He that waits for a dead man's shoes may go barefoot long.

* How beautiful is it to do nothing, and then rest afterward.

* Waiting for a rabbit to hit a tree and be killed in order to catch it. [Chinese]

* There are no better masters than poverty and

wants. [Dutch]

* If any would not work, neither should he eat.

* A curled snake never gets fat. [Liberia]

* Laziness weakens the hand.

LEADERSHIP

* A glorious past is the work of a glorious man.

* Among the blind, the one eyed is king.

* An army of deer would be more formidable (hard to handle) commanded by a lion, than an army of lions commanded by a stag (full-grown male deer).

* Govern a family as you would cook a small fish; very gently. [Chinese]

* Power lasts ten years; influence not more than a hundred. [Korean]

* Practice what you preach.

* Precept guides, but example draws.

* The counsel you would have another keep, first keep yourself.

* The eye of the master does more than both his hands.

* The king goes as far as he may, not as far as he could.

* When a king has good counsellors, his reign is

peaceful.

❀ The lead cow (the one in front) gets whipped the most. [South Africa]

❀ The nail that sticks up will be hammered down.

❀ He who knows the way must conduct others. [Liberia]

❀ When elephants fight the grass gets hurt. [Kenya] (*leaders disputes and divisions end up hurting innocent and powerless people*)

❀ He who steps in (a river) first shows the depth of the current. [Liberia]

LONELINESS

❀ Distant water won't help to put out a fire close at hand. [Chinese]

❀ Loneliness breaks the spirit. [Jewish]

❀ He who eats alone chokes alone.

LOVE

❀ If you love it let it go; if it returns to you cherish it, if not, it was never truly yours.

❀ Love can neither be bought nor sold; its only price is love.

❀ Love sees no faults.

❀ Perfect love cannot be without equality.

❀ When an only kola nut is presented with love, it carries with it more value than might; otherwise, be associated with a whole pod of several kola nuts.

❀ The death of the heart is the saddest thing that can happen to you.

❀ "Flog my erring child" comes from the lips; "don't hurt him/her" comes from the bottom of the heart.

❀ Love is better than a whip.

❀ A man in love mistakes a pimple for a dimple.

❀ In love, there is always one who kisses and one who offers the cheek.

❀ Love is blind. **[Sierra Leone]**

❀ Love is like war; easy to begin, hard to end.

❀ Love makes time pass away and time makes love pass away.

❀ Never love with all your heart, it only ends in breaking.

❀ One does not love if one does not accept from others. [**Nigeria**]

❀ Our love is like the misty rain that falls softly, but floods the river.

❀ The heart that truly loves never forgets.

❀ What the eyes does not admire, the heart does not desire.

❀ Whoever the heart loves, she is the beauty.

* Love me little, love me long.

LOYALTY

* Masters who sacrifice for servants will receive the gift of loyalty.

* No man can serve two masters.

LUCK

* A good fortune may forebode a bad luck, which may in turn disguise a good fortune.

* It is better to be lucky than rich.

* Luck is infatuated with the efficient.

* Luck seeks those who flee and flees those who seek it.

* The unexpected always happens.

* Throw a lucky man into the sea and he will come up with a fish in his mouth.

* You cannot take away someone's luck. [**Kenya**]

* You cannot expect both ends of a sugar cane are as sweet.

* You do not need intelligence to have luck, but you do need luck to have intelligence.

M

MARRIAGE

* Marriage is the sunset of love.

* Marrying is easy; it's housework that's hard.

* Those that marry for money sell their liberty.

* Wedlock is padlock.

* Choose your wife as you wish your children to be.

* Marriage is a lottery.

* Marriage is like a besieged castle; those who are on the outside wish to get in, and those who are on the inside wish to get out.

* One's best fortune, or their worst, is their spouse.

* The day you marry, it is either kill or cure.

* Never marry for money, but marry where the money is.

* A woman who is not successful in her own marriage has no advice to give to her younger generations.

* He who marries a real beauty is seeking trouble. [Ghana]

MEDDLESOME

* Do not be concerned with things outside your door.

* There are always ears on the other side of the wall.

* Of what does not concern you, say nothing good or bad.

* Everybody's business is nobody's business.

MEEKNESS / HUMILITY

* Confess you were wrong yesterday; it will show you are wise today.

* Even though you know a thousand things, ask the man who knows one.

* He who refuses to obey cannot command.

* If two ride a horse, one must ride behind.

* Singing 'hallelujah' everywhere does not prove piety devotion to religious duties.

* The fowl perspires, but the feathers do not allow us to see the perspiration.

* Where you will sit when you are old, shows where you stood in youth.

* How can man be remembered when the giant trees in the forest are soon forgotten.

* However much the world degenerates, man

shall never find worms in salt.

❀ From small beginnings come great things.

❀ If you can walk, you can dance; if you can talk, you can sing.

MONEY

❀ A broke man goes through the market fast.

❀ Where gold speaks every tongue is silent.

❀ The love of money is the root of all evil.

❀ Money spent on the mind is never spent in vain.

❀ Money is flat and meant to be piled up.

❀ A penny is a lot of money, if you have not got a penny.

❀ Getting money is like digging with a needle, spending it is like water soaking into sand. [Japanese]

MOURNING

❀ Grief is light that is capable of counsel.

N

NEVER GIVE UP

* The back of one door is the face of another.

* One must row in whichever boat one finds one's self.

* It is better to light one candle than to curse the darkness.

* Better to bend in the wind than to break.

* Do not vacillate (sway) or you will be left in between doing something, having something and being nothing. [**Ethiopian**]

* Down seven times, get up eight. [**Japanese**]

* It is better to walk than curse the road. [**Senegal**]

* Little by little a bird builds its nest.

* Smooth seas do not make skilful sailors.

* To try and to fail is not laziness.

* When one is taking a chicken from its roost, the hen is bound to attack with at least its claws .

* God may still send a gentle breeze when He wants to bless us.

O

OLD AGE

* As you see yourself, I once saw myself; as you see me now, you will be seen.

* Even a friend cannot rescue one from old age. [Kenya]

* I came to the place of my birth and cried, "The friends of my youth, where are they?" An echo answered, "Where are they?"

* I have come a long way; the journey has exhausted me. [Tanzania] (*the typical situation of an aged person who has lived for many years have faced many hurdles*)

* Man fools himself; he prays for a long life and he fears old age.

* An old woman is always uneasy when dry bones are mentioned in a proverb.

* Old age does not come in just one day.

* One must have to wait till the evening of one's life time to know what gratitude to pay to one's guardian angel.

* There is no medicine against old age. [Ghana]

* Old age, though despised, is coveted by all.

* They that live longest, see most.

* Never too old to learn.

* When a palm-branch reaches its height, it gives way for a fresh one to grow.

* What an elder sees sitting, the young cannot see standing. [**Nigeria**]

* Elders choose their words. [**Kenya**]

OPPORTUNITY

* One man's difficulty is another's opportunity.

* Opportunity makes a thief.

* Neglected opportunities can never be recovered.

* Opportunity seldom knocks twice.

* Four things never come back; the spoken word, the sped arrow, the past life and the neglected opportunity.

* When fortune knocks, open the door.

P

PARENTING

* A hundred men may make an encampment, but it takes a woman to make a home.

* One generation plants the tree; another gets the shade. [Chinese]

* Send a boy where he wants to go and you will see his best pace.

* If you educate a man you educate an individual, but if you educate a woman, you educate a family. [Ghana]

* A person who is not disciplined cannot be cautioned. [Tanzania]

* Young growing cuttings determine a good harvest of cassava [Malawi]

PATIENCE

* Hasty climbers have sudden falls.

* Moderate profits fill the purse.

* After hardship, comes relief.

* By persevering, the egg walks on legs (*patience enables one to succeed*).

* Diligence is the mother of good luck.

* Don't insult the hunting guide before the sun has set. [**Tanzania**]

* He who is slow to anger has great understanding, but he who has a hasty temper exalts folly.

* However long the night, the dawn will break.

* Hurrying and worrying are not the same as strength.

* If you are patient in one moment of anger, you will escape a hundred days of sorrow.

* Patience can cook a stone.

* Patience is bitter, but its fruit is sweet.

* Patience is power; with time and patience the mulberry leaf becomes a silk gown. [**Chinese**]

* Patience is the key which solves all problems. [**Sudan**]

* There is no bad patience.

* An ounce of practice is worth a pound of preaching.

* Step by step, one goes very far.

* The difficult is done at once, the impossible takes a little longer.

* God delays but doesn't forget.

* A gem is not polished without rubbing, nor a man perfected without trials.

✿ A speedy wrestling and a bad fall go hand in hand.

✿ Distance tests the endurance of a horse; time reveals a man's character.

✿ However long, the moon disappears, someday it must shine again.

✿ It is not only the hare, the tortoise arrives also at the destination.

✿ One does not become a master diviner in a day.

✿ A forest is not made in a season.

✿ The swoop of an eagle has seen many seasons and floods.

✿ Patient people are patient to gain longevity.

✿ The thirsty fig sits waiting patiently, waiting for the arrival of the rains.

✿ Wait long, strike fast.

✿ It is the same moon that wanes today that will be the full moon tomorrow.

✿ It is only the toad that gets up from its knees and falls back again on its knees.

✿ The spider that knows what it will gain sits waiting patiently in its web.

✿ The praying mantis is never tired waiting all day.

✿ Who says the oasis in the desert is happy because of its hidden spring of water?

* The cricket is never blinded by the sand of its burrowing.

* An oil lamp feels proud to give light even though it wears itself away.

* A bird does not change its feathers because the weather is bad.

* A full cup must be carried steadily.

* A watched pot never boils.

* All is not lost that is delayed.

* By coming and going, a bird weaves its nest. [Ghana]

* For what cannot be cured, patience is best.

* Patience can conquer destiny.

* Patience is a plaster for all sores.

* Patience is a virtue that causes no shame.

* Patience, money and time bring all things to past.

* Patience, when teased, is often transformed into rage.

* Stairs are climbed step by step.

* The one who waits the fine day, will get the fine day.

* Time is a great healer.

* Time works wonders.

* Be not afraid of growing slowly; be afraid only

of standing still.

❀ Tomorrow makes known to us what tomorrow will bring.

❀ A 'hurry-hurry' person eats goat; the one who takes his time eats beef

❀ Haste is from the Devil.

PATRIOTISM / LOYALTY

❀ A bush fowl's playground is never noticeably spacious.

❀ Even when fire has done its very worst, one still has to resort to it.

❀ Everyone praises his native land.

❀ If the owner of a calabash calls it a worthless calabash, others will join him to use it to pack rubbish.

❀ The ruin of a nation begins in the homes of its people.

❀ No elephant is burdened by the weight of its tusks.

❀ What affects the nose must also affect the eyes that must weep for it.

❀ When a soup is unpalatable, and the paste of the pounded yam that goes with it is not smooth, that is the time to know a man who loves to eat pounded yam. [**Nigeria**]

PEACE

❀ Great is the victory that is gained without bloodshed.

❀ He who forgives, ends the argument.

❀ Leave bad things, talk peace. [Kenya]

❀ Make peace with man and war with your sins.

❀ One can not reflect in streaming water. Only those who know internal peace can give it to others.

❀ Peace is costly, but it is worth the expense.

❀ Peace is worth buying.

❀ Smoke does not affect honeybees alone; honey-gatherers are also affected. [Liberia]

❀ The tree of silence bears the fruit of peace.

❀ To agree to have dialogue is the beginning of a peaceful resolution. [Somali]

❀ War is not food [Kenya]

❀ When we cannot find peace in ourselves, it is vain to look for it elsewhere.

❀ Where there is peace, a billhook (sickle) can be used to shave your beard or cut your hair. [Burundi]

❀ Peace only comes when reason rules.

❀ A spacious ground is the right place to demonstrate one's skill in wrestling.

❀ If the owner of two adjacent farms cannot be friends, then they must wait till their next reincarnation to be able to make friends.

❀ "Let's fight, let's fight," no one knows whom fighting would favor.

❀ To have no enemies is equivalent to wealth.

❀ Two men quarreling do not share the same seat on a canoe.

❀ When a man finds that he was wrong to have refused to eat, he should leave his anger and play a harp to call for harmony.

❀ Whoever says "let's fight" does not know who will be victorious.

❀ Without retaliation evil would one day become extinct from the world.

❀ No matter who succeeds or fails, the peacemaker will always suffer.

POLITICS

❀ Politics makes strange bedfellows.

POVERTY

❀ An advantage of poverty; your relatives gain nothing by your death.

❀ Painless poverty is better than embittered wealth.

* Poverty is a wonderful thing; it sticks to a man after all his friends have forsaken him.

* Poverty is not a shame, but the being ashamed of it, is.

* Poverty is slavery. [**Somalia**]

* True poverty does not come from God.

* When poverty comes in at the door, love flies out of the window.

* Quickly come, quickly go.

* Poverty has no greater foe than bashfulness.

POWER

* If power is for sale, sell your mother to buy it; you can always buy her back again.

* Persuasion is better than force.

* Power corrupts.

* That fear may reach all, punish but few.

* Power lasts ten years; influence not more than a hundred.

* The lion does not turn around when a small dog bark.

PRAISE

* Everyone speaks well of the bridge which carries him over.

❀ Praise makes good people better and bad people worse.

❀ Praise the child, and you make love to the mother.

❀ The best way to get praise is to die.

❀ While a person gets, they can never lose.

PREPARATION

❀ A rich child often sits in a poor mother's lap.

❀ Sunday well-spent brings a week of content.

❀ All wealth begins in the mind.

❀ Be on the alert, like the red ant that moves with its claws wide open. [Uganda]

❀ Could anything be done twice, it would be done better.

❀ Do they prepare leather for a battle shield the day they fight? [Nigeria]

❀ Every man is the architect of his own fortune.

❀ First secure an independent income, and then practice virtue.

❀ It is best to be off with the old love before you are on with the new.

❀ One hour's sleep before midnight is worth two after.

❀ Prevention is better than cure.

* Rising early makes the road short. [**Senegal**]

* Tomorrow belongs to the people who prepare for it today.

* When you are dying of thirst, it's too late to think about digging a well.

PRIDE

* If you are filled with pride, then you will have no room for wisdom. [**Tanzania**]

* No one is as angry as the person who is wrong.

* People blame themselves for the purpose of being praised.

* The owl of ignorance lays the egg of pride.

* A proud heart can survive a general failure; because such a failure does not prick its pride.

* Pride and poverty don't get along, but often live together.

* A proud heart can survive a general failure because such a failure does not prick its pride.

* If a man is not clean and smooth, there is nothing he can really do about pride.

* It is nice to be important, but it is more important to be nice.

* A man cannot be taller than his head. [**Liberia**]

PROCRASTINATION

* Age and time do not wait for people.

* Delays are dangerous.

* He loses his thanks who promises and delays.

* He who hesitates is lost.

* One of these days, is none of these days.

* Procrastination is the thief of time.

* Punctuality is the soul of business.

* Ready money works great cures.

* The first step is the hardest.

* Tomorrow never comes.

* We are not so much concerned if you are slow as when you come to a halt.

* We hate delays by others, but sometimes it makes us wise.

* While we keep a man waiting, he reflects on our shortcomings.

* Why kill time when you can employ it.

* Now, is the watchword of the wise.

R

REALITY CHECK

❧ It is better than you think.

❧ It is the truth that irritates a person.

❧ Since we cannot get what we like, let us like what we can get.

❧ Take the world as it is, not as it ought to be. [German]

❧ The sky is not less blue because the blind man does not see it.

❧ Water cannot be forced uphill. [Kenya]

❧ Wide will wear; tight will tear.

❧ You cannot force anyone to love you or lend you money.

❧ It is when there is a stampede, that a person with big buttocks knows that he carries a load.

❧ A crowd is like a smoldering log, which can spark into a flame at any time.

❧ A good lawyer is a bad neighbor.

❧ A hungry man is an angry man.

❧ A hungry stomach has no ears.

❀ A lizard that fell from the top of a tree wastes its time looking back to where it fell from; if there was anything good the lizard deserved, it could not have missed it while it was there on top of the tree.

❀ A misty morning does not signify a cloudy day.

❀ A psychic cannot accurately divine his own future.

❀ A single spark can set a prairie on fire.

❀ A tiger never returns to his prey he did not finish off.

❀ An inch of time cannot be bought with an inch of gold.

❀ At a time a cockerel matures, it begins to crow to tell the world the time of day.

❀ Battle doesn't need a purpose; the battle is its own purpose.

❀ Even a worm will turn.

❀ Even the tallest tower started from the ground.

❀ Even the tallest tree has an ax waiting at its foot.

❀ Evil doers are evil dreaders.

❀ For every wise man, there is one still wiser.

❀ Great thieves punish little ones.

❀ He who begins and does not finish loves their pains.

❧ If a dog's prayers were answered, bones would rain from the sky.

❧ In time of trouble, leniency (tolerance) becomes a crime.

❧ It is easy to say, 'come'; difficult to say, 'go'

❧ It is the long lane that has no turning.

❧ Let rats shoot arrows at each other.

❧ Never do anything standing that you can do sitting, or anything sitting that you can do lying down.

❧ Never offer to teach a fish to swim.

❧ No smoke without fire.

❧ Nothing is nobler than politeness, and nothing is more ridiculous than ceremony.

❧ Of all the stratagem (trick), to know when to quit is the best.

❧ Offenders never pardon.

❧ Old habits die hard.

❧ Once a cock begins to crow, it never again becomes dumb.

❧ Once you pour the water out of the bucket, it's hard to get it back in it. [**Chinese**]

❧ Paper cannot wrap up a fire.

❧ Sometimes you must be cruel to be kind.

❧ Straws tell which way the wind blows.

* The exception proves the rule.

* The hardest work of all is to do nothing.

* The multitude is always wrong.

* The palest ink lasts longer than the most retentive memory. [**Chinese**]

* The rainmaker who does not know what he is doing will be found out by the lack of clouds. [**Uganda**]

* The shoemaker's son always goes barefoot.

* The shortest answer is doing.

* The silent dog is the first to bite.

* The third time pays for all.

* There are no birds in last year's nest.

* There is nothing new, but what has become antiquated.

* Times change, and we with time.

* To every cow its calf; to every book its copy.

* What is new cannot be true.

* What must be must be.

* When we have nothing to worry about, we are not doing much; and not doing much may supply us with plenty of future worries. [**Chinese**]

* Where the rooster crows, there is a village.

* Wish well, be well.

* You are sitting in peace (unharmed) as the nose of a cow that feeds among thorn trees and shows no scars. [Uganda]

* You cannot make omelets without breaking eggs.

* The poor man's budget is full of schemes.

* To call 'war' the soil of courage and virtue is like calling 'debauchery' the soil of love.

* When you live next to the cemetery, you cannot weep for everyone.

RESPECT

* A hundred years cannot repair a moment's loss of honor.

* Civility (politeness) costs nothing.

* Respect for ones parents is the highest duty of civil life. [Chinese]

REWARD

* One good turn deserves another.

* Speedy exception is the mother of good fortune.

* The end crowns the work.

* The end of a feast is better than the beginning of a fight.

RICHES

❀ A rich widow weeps with one eye and signals with the other.

❀ Riches have wings.

❀ When you are rich, you are hated; when you are poor, you are despised.

❀ He who loves money must labor.

❀ If the rich could hire other people to die for them, the poor could make a wonderful living.

❀ If you have money, men think you are wise, handsome, and able to sing like a bird.

❀ If you want to know what God thinks of money, look at the people He gives it to.

❀ Marry for money, my little sonny; a rich man's joke is always funny.

❀ Money is sharper than the sword. [Ghana]

❀ When you are poor, neighbors close by will not come; once you become rich, you'll be surprised by visits from (alleged) relatives afar. [Chinese]

❀ A rich man has no need of character.

❀ After a rich man gets rich, his next ambition is to get richer.

❀ The poor man and the rich man do not play together. [Ghana]

❀ Riches; a dream in the night. Fame; a gull floating on water. [Chinese]

S

SECRET

❀ Confiding a secret to an unworthy person is like carrying grain in a bag with a hole.

❀ Nothing is as burdensome as a secret.

❀ The bush in which you hind, has eyes [**Kenya**]

SELFISHNESS

❀ It is easy to catch a serpent with someone else's hand.

❀ It's ill speaking between a full man and a fasting.

❀ Who spits against the wind, spits in his own face.

❀ The person who has eaten and satisfied himself does not care for the one who is hungry. [**Tanzania**]

❀ The stones that you throw into the well to kill frogs are the same stones that will cause you to suffer when you drink the dirty water. [**Liberia**]

SELFLESSNESS

❀ The hen with baby chicks doesn't swallow the worm. [Tanzania]

❀ He that plants trees loves others besides himself.

❀ The charitable give out the door and God puts it back through the window.

❀ The soul is not where it lives, but where it loves.

❀ The spirit of man is the candle of the Lord.

❀ The sun loses nothing by shining into a puddle.

❀ You do good, you do good for yourself.

STUBBORNNESS

❀ No one is as deaf as the man who will not listen.

❀ There's none so deaf as those who will not hear.

❀ Who God wishes to destroy, He first makes mad.

❀ A child does not fear treading on dangerous ground until he gets hurt. [Kenya]

❀ If you refuse the elder's advice, you will walk the whole day. [Tanzania]

❀ A stubborn person sails in a clay boat. [Tanzania]

SUCCESS

* Substance is not enough, accident is also required.

* The darkest hour is just before the dawn.

* Think of many things, do only one.

* To believe a thing is impossible is to make it so.

* When difficulties are overcome, they begin blessing.

* The highway to failure is smooth, but the road to success is constantly under construction.

* Your highest accomplishment may come from your deepest suffering.

SURVIVAL

* The frog does not run in the daytime for nothing.

* Though the lion and the antelope happen to live in the same forest, the antelope still has time to grow up. [Ghana]

* You cannot prevent the birds of sorrow from flying over your head, but you can prevent them from building nests in your hair. [Chinese]

* A child does not die because the mother's breasts are dry.

❀ If the load is too heavy for someone to carry, one would be better off to give the load to the ground to carry.

❀ It is the toothless animal that arrives first at the base of the fruit tree, to eat his fill before others arrive.

❀ The tree that cannot shed its old leaves in the dry season, cannot survive the period of drought.

SYMPATHY

❀ Pity is akin to love.

❀ No one feels the pains that arise from unintended injury.

T

TAKING RISKS

❀ Biggest profits mean gravest risks.

❀ Danger and delight grow on one stalk.

❀ Every bad has its worst.

❀ Every convenience brings its own inconveniences along with it.

* If you don't make mistakes, you don't make anything.

* Never is a long time.

* No matter where you go, your destiny follows you.

* One who is crazy for meat hunts buffalo. [Uganda]

* That, which proves too much, proves nothing.

* There is no greater misfortune, than to not be able to endure misfortune.

* There is nothing certain but the uncertain.

* Try and trust will never move mountains.

* We should put out fire while it is still small. [Kenya]

* Who buys cheap, buys dear.

* Who never climbed, never fell.

* You cannot lose what you never had.

TALKATIVE

* A chattering bird builds no nest.

* A closed mouth catches no flies.

* A dog that barks much is never a good hunter.

* A still tongue makes a wise head.

* Truth spoken before its time is dangerous.

❀ At table, keep a short hand; in company, keep a short tongue.

❀ From listening comes wisdom and from speaking, repentance.

❀ He bites his tongue who speaks in haste.

❀ He who talks incessantly, talks nonsense.

❀ If you wish to know the mind of a man, listen to his words.

❀ In the midst of great joy, do not promise anyone anything; in the midst of great anger, do not answer anyone's letter. [Chinese]

❀ Out of the fullness of the heart, the mouth speaks.

❀ People who have little to do are excessive talkers.

❀ Speaking comes by nature, silence by understanding.

❀ Talk well of your friends and of your enemies, say nothing.

❀ The less people think, the more they talk.

❀ The owl is the wisest of all birds; the more it sees, the less it talks.

❀ The tongue always returns to the sore tooth.

❀ The tongue can paint what the eye can't see.

❀ Those who know do not talk; those who talk do not know.

* To talk without thinking is to shoot without aiming.

* Two great talkers will not travel far together.

* When your mouth stumbles, it's worse than feet.

* Who knows much says least.

* Talk little; listen much. [**Mauritanian**]

* The goat that cries the loudest is not the one that will eat the most.

* There are two things over which you have complete dominion, authority and control; your mind and your mouth.

TEACHING

* Giving your son a skill is better than giving him one thousand pieces of gold.

* Good advice is beyond all price.

* Tell me, I'll forget, show me and I may remember, involve me and I'll understand.

* Whatever you teach, be brief; what is quickly said, the mind readily receives and faithfully retains, while everything superfluous runs over as from a full container.

* To teach well, we need not say all that we know.

* When planning for a year, plant corn; when planning for a decade, plant trees; when planning for life, train and educate people.

❀ Talks that are considered to be important must be made to drag on for so long as to make even the deaf begin to hear it.

TEAMWORK

❀ Watching is a part of good play.

❀ Unity is strength. [Uganda]

❀ "Go in that direction" does not mean that you go; to go means, "Let's go together!"

❀ Two ants do not fail to pull one grasshopper. [Tanzania]

❀ It is by the strength of their number that the ants in the field are able to carry their prey to the nest.

❀ One finger cannot remove lice from the head.

❀ One hand alone cannot clap.

❀ One sings, all follow.

❀ Two footsteps do not make a path.

❀ Two raindrops do not make a pool.

❀ One bee makes no swarm.

❀ One man in the field is not a warrior.

❀ One head does not contain all the wisdom. [Ghana]

TEMPERANCE

* A clay pot of water is never hot-tempered.

* Don't' holler till you are out of the wood.

* Less is more.

* Listen a hundred times; ponder a thousand times; speak once.

* Moderations in all things.

* Spare well and have to spend.

* What you have, hold.

THOUGHTFULNESS

* A knife-wound heals, but a tongue wound festers.

* If I keep a green bough in my heart, the singing bird will come. [Chinese]

* Never speak of a rope in the family of one who has been hanged.

* Once a word leaves your mouth, you cannot chase it back even with the swiftest horse. [Chinese]

* The mother-in-law remembers not that she was a daughter-in-law.

* Use soft words and hard arguments.

* A cutting word is worse than a bowstring, a cut may heal, but the cut of the tongue does not.

* A fowl does not forget where it lays its eggs.

* A person, who does not bathe, must know it of himself that he is dirty.

* All truth is good, but all truth is not good to say.

* Anyone who urinates in a stream should be warned, any of his relatives may drink from the water.

* Ashes fly back into the face of him who throws them.

* Before shooting, one must aim.

* Does a man not know when he has pepper in his eyes? If we forget yesterday, how shall we remember tomorrow?

* Drinking the water of a well, one should never forget who dug it.

* Even as the archer loves the arrow that flies, so too he loves the bow that remains constant in his hands.

* He who is being carried does not realize how far the town is.

* It is one word of advice that one needs to give to a wise man, and that word keeps multiplying in his mind.

* Provided no person stunts or destroys a sprouting palm kernel seedling, it will definitely grow into a palm tree. [Nigeria]

* Quarrels end, but words once spoken never

die.

* Tears of the orphan run inside. [**West Africa**]

* Whether the knife falls on the melon or the melon on the knife, the melon suffers.

* Wood already touched by fire is not hard to set alight.

* Words are like bullets; if they escape, you cannot catch them again. [**Gambia**] *Be quick to listen, slow to speak, and slow to get angry)*

* You cannot use a wild banana leaf to shield yourself from the rain and then tear it to pieces later when the rain comes to an end. [**Kenya**]

* Judge a man by the work of his hands.

TIMING

* Many will show you the way once your cart has overturned.

* All things grow with time, except grief.

* Time and I against any two.

* Time heals old pain, while it creates new ones.

* The right man comes at the right time.

* When it is the turn of a man to become the head of a village, he does not need the mind reader to tell him that he is destined to rule.

* When the fruit is ripe, it will fall.

TRADITION

* Custom is a tyrant.

* If you don't know where you come from, you cannot know where you are going. [**Nigeria**]

TRUST

* It is an equal, failing to trust everybody and to trust nobody.

* If you suspect a man, don't employ him; and if you employ him, don't suspect him. [**Chinese**]

* Never trust the man who tells you all his troubles but keeps from you all his joys.

* Where there is no trust, there is no love.

W

WEALTH

* Beetles that roll balls out of human feces demand to be hidden away from the rich man, because there is nothing he wouldn't buy.

* If you are poor, though you dwell in the busy marketplace, no one will inquire about you; if you are rich, though you dwell in the heart of

the mountains, you will have distant relatives. [**Chinese**]

❁ If you want one year of prosperity, grow grain; if you want ten years of prosperity, grow trees; if you want one hundred years of prosperity, grow people. [**Chinese**]

❁ Of the wealth of the world, each has as much as they take.

❁ What you spend, you have.

❁ What you've never had, you never miss.

❁ A great fortune depends on luck, a small one on diligence. [**Chinese**]

❁ A man's wealth may be superior to him. [**Cameroon**]

❁ Fortune has a fickle heart and a short memory.

❁ We brought nothing into this world, and it is certain we can carry nothing out.

WISDOM

❁ The habit of thinking is the habit of gaining strength.

❁ We are what our thinking makes us.

❁ Thoughts and dreams are the foundation of our being.

❁ A messenger cannot be beaten. [**Kenya**]

❁ A single conversation across the table with

a wise man is worth a month's study of books. [**Chinese**]

❧ A windy day is not the day for thatching. [**Irish**]

❧ Any landing you can walk away from is a good one.

❧ Better a friendly refusal than an unwilling consent.

❧ Brevity (the quality of being brief) is the soul of wit (power of thinking and reasoning).

❧ By others faults the wise correct their own.

❧ Drink nothing without seeing it; sign nothing without reading it. [**Spanish**]

❧ Education begins a gentleman, conversation completes him. [**English**]

❧ A rising tide lifts all boats.

❧ Hope for the best, but prepare for the worst.

❧ No man limps because another is hurt.

❧ Office without pay makes thieves.

❧ Pay beforehand, if you would have your work poorly done.

❧ Simplicity is the seal of truth.

❧ That which is escaped now, is pain to come.

❧ The beginning of wisdom is to call things by their right names.

❀ The crows, the idle person grumbles. [Nigeria]

❀ Treat your superior as a father, your equal as a brother and your inferior as a son.

❀ What you don't see with your eyes, don't witness with your mouth. [Jewish]

❀ Wise men do not quarrel with each other.

❀ You cannot please everyone.

❀ A book is like a garden carried in the pocket.

❀ A cat in gloves catches no mice.

❀ A change is as good as a rest.

❀ A closed mind is like a closed book, just a block of wood.

❀ A crane standing amidst a flock of chickens. [Chinese]

❀ A hero is a man who is afraid to run away.

❀ A hyena cannot smell its own stench. [Kenya]

❀ A low-class man will just talk; deeds are the hallmark of a gentleman.

❀ A great man never puts away the simplicity of a child.

❀ A sly rabbit will have three openings to its den.

❀ A small key opens big doors.

❀ A stranger does not skin a sheep that is paid as a fine at a chief's court. [Ghana]

❀ A stumble may prevent a fall.

❀ A wise man does his own work.

❀ A wise man hears one word and understands two.

❀ A wise man never knows all, only fools know everything.

❀ A word from the mouth is like a stone from a sling.

❀ Act quickly, think slowly.

❀ Acts of kindness may soon be forgotten, but the memory of an offense remains.

❀ Add legs to the snake after you have finished drawing it.

❀ An old error is always more popular than a new truth.

❀ An open book benefits your mind.

❀ Art is long; life is short.

❀ At a round table, there is no dispute about place.

❀ Better a lean agreement than a fat lawsuit.

❀ Better to ask a question than to remain ignorant.

❀ Better to be envied than pitied.

❀ Butcher the donkey after it finished his job on the mill. [**Chinese**]

❀ By doing nothing we learn to do ill.

* By learning you will teach, by teaching you will learn.

* Carelessness is worse than a thief.

* Change yourself; change your fortunes.

* Circumstances alter cases.

* Councils of war never flight.

* Curses are like chickens, they always come home.

* Do not boast about yourself before performing an event, but after the event. [Kenya]

* Do not call to a dog with a whip in your hand.

* Do not confine your children to your own learning, for they were born in another time.

* Do not follow a person who is running away. [Kenya]

* Do not meet trouble half way.

* Don't cross the bridge till you come to it.

* Don't throw away the old bucket until you know whether the new one holds water.

* Dream different dreams while on the same bed. [Chinese]

* Every animal knows more than you do.

* Facts come by means of jokes.

* Fear the man who fears you.

* First attain skill; creativity comes later.

* Flies never visit an egg that has no crack.

* Forever is a long bargain.

* Great oaks, from little acorns grow.

* He flees from a roaring lion to the crouching lion.

* He that asks what he should not, hears what he would not.

* He that jokes, confesses.

* He that parts with the property before his death, prepares himself for much suffering.

* He that seeks trouble never misses.

* He, who is not satisfied with himself, will not grow.

* He, who learns, teaches.

* He who puts up with insult invites injury.

* He, who strikes first, strikes twice.

* If he works for you, you work for him. [**Japanese**]

* If the doctor cures, the sun sees it; if he kills, the earth hides it.

* If we do not change our directions, we are likely to end up where we are headed.

* If you cannot be good, be careful.

* If you don't speculate, you cannot accumulate.

* If you want an audience start a fight.

❀ If your cornfield is far from your house, the birds will eat your corn.

❀ If your strength is small, don't carry heavy burdens; if your words are worthless, don't give advice.

❀ If you want your dream to come true, don't over sleep.

❀ In teaching others, we teach ourselves.

❀ In the morning of life, work; in the mid day, give council; in the evening, pray.

❀ Indecision is like a stepchild; if he does not wash his hands, he is called dirty, if he does, he is wasting water.

❀ I dreamed a thousand new paths; I woke and walked my old one. [**Chinese**]

❀ I hear and I forget, I see and I remember, I do and I understand. [**Chinese**]

❀ It is better to run back than run the wrong way.

❀ It is more difficult to contend with oneself than with the world.

❀ It is not necessary to light a candle to the sun.

❀ It is nothing for one to know something unless another knows you know it.

❀ It's all very well in practice, but it will never work in theory.

❀ It's no use carrying an umbrella if your shoes are leaking.

❀ Kings have many ears and eyes.

❀ Laughing is not always the proof of a mind at ease.

❀ Learning is like the horizon; there is no limit.

❀ Life is a bridge; cross over it, but build no house on it.

❀ Like ants, eat little and carry the rest back to your home. [**Tanzania**]

❀ Live to live and you will learn to live.

❀ Live today for tomorrow it will all be history.

❀ Make the cap fit the head.

❀ Many may bear adversity, but few, contempt.

❀ Measure three times before you cut once.

❀ Men in the game are blind, men outside see clearly.

❀ Necessity is the mother of invention.

❀ Never advise anyone to go to war or to get married.

❀ Never give advice unless asked.

❀ Never step over one duty to perform another.

❀ Never wrestle with a strong man nor bring a rich man to court.

❀ No answer is also an answer.

❀ No one know how the poor man dines.

* Nobody kills an ignorant person who begs for wisdom. [**Nigeria**]

* Nothing weights lighter than a promise.

* Of all the thirty-six alternatives, running away is best.

* One chops the wood, the other does the grunting.

* One flower will make a garland (wreath-a symbol of victory).

* One may survive distress, but not disgrace.

* Our elders quote the cock as saying that "it would not be good if one becomes the only person in the world, and that is why they crow every morning to show their number".

* Our examples are like seeds on a windy day, they spread far and wide.

* Pain is only weakness leaving the body.

* Pleasure for one hour, a bottle of wine; pleasure for one year, a marriage; but pleasure for a lifetime, a garden. [**Chinese**]

* Pray that you will never have to bear all that you are able to endure. [Jewish]

* Reason is the wise man's guide, example the fool's.

* Reason lies between the bridle and the spur.

* Repentance won't cure mischief.

* Shame is worse than death.

* Short lived pleasure is the parent of pain.

* Something you do not want is dear at any price.

* Stumbling is not falling.

* Tell the truth and then run.

* The believer is happy; the doubter is wise.

* The best counselors are the dead.

* The best throw of the dice is to throw them away.

* The bread never falls but on its buttered side.

* The buyer needs a hundred eyes; the seller but one.

* The day that monkey is destined to die, all the trees get slippery.

* The dog does not worry when the chicken runs over to the bones. [Ghana]

* The end justifies the means.

* The eyes of a wise man see through you. [Tanzania]

* The first mistake are theirs who commit them, the second is theirs that permit them.

* The good fellow to everyone is a good friend to no one.

* The haughty blind person picks a fight with his guide. [Ethiopian]

* The healthy die first.

* The journey of a thousand miles must begin with a single step. [Chinese]

* The morning hour has gold in its mouth.

* The one who fetches the water is the one who is likely to break the pot. [Ghana]

* The one who pleased everybody died before they were born.

* The one who wills is the one who can.

* The orphan does not rejoice after a heavy breakfast. [Ghana]

* The pants of today are better than the breeches of tomorrow [Burkina Faso]

* The person who fights and runs away will live to fight another battle. [Sudan] (*there is a time and reason not to fight / discretion is the better part of valor*)

* The sun does not forget a village just because it is small.

* The superior doctor prevents sickness; the mediocre doctor attends to impending sickness; the inferior doctor treats actual sickness. [Chinese]

* Those who have free seats at a play are first. [Chinese]

* To advise is not to compel.

* To aim is not enough, but must hit.

* To be uncertain is to be uncomfortable, but to be certain is to be ridiculous. [Chinese]

❀ To punch with a strong fist, you need to turn over your hand. [**Angola**]

❀ To read a book for the first time is to make an acquaintance with a new friend; to read it for a second time, is to meet an old one.

❀ Too much zeal spoils everything.

❀ Travel broadens the mind.

❀ Unwilling service earns no thanks.

❀ Use of brains begets wealth. [**Kenya**]

❀ Wait until it is night before saying that it has been a fine day.

❀ Walk on a fresh tree, the dry one will break. [**Tanzania**]

❀ Water can both sustain and sink a ship.

❀ We add wisdom to knowledge. [**Kenya**]

❀ We know the true worth of a thing when we have lost it.

❀ What is in the stomach carries what is in the head. [**Kenya**]

❀ What is not yours always chirps for its master. [**Spanish**]

❀ What soap is to the body, tears are for the soul.

❀ What the lion cannot manage to do, the fox can.

❀ What you cannot see during the day, you will not see at night.

❀ Whatever accomplishment you boast of in the world, there is someone better than you.

❀ When a fire starts from the shrine, no precaution can be possible.

❀ When a man is coming toward you, you need not say 'come here'.

❀ When a tree falls on a yam farm and kills the farm owner, you do not waste time counting the numbers of yam hips ruined. [**Nigeria**]

❀ When a woman prepares a dish which others find unpalatable, she says that she prepared it to suit her own taste.

❀ When danger approaches, sing to it.

❀ When an elephant steps on a trap, no more trap.

❀ When the sun rises, it rises for everyone.

❀ When you reach the top of the Mountain, climb higher!

❀ Willful waste makes woeful want.

❀ Wisdom is like a baobab tree; no one individual can embrace it. [**Akan & Ewe**]

❀ Who walks in front gives you wisdom. [**Uganda**]

❀ If you climb up a tree, you must climb down the same tree.

❀ Wisdom is like fire; people take it from others. [**Democratic Republic of Congo**]

❀ You cannot catch a cub without going into a tiger's den. [Chinese]

❀ Zeal is like fire; it needs both feed and watching.

❀ A wise man who knows proverbs, reconciles difficulties. [Ghana]

❀ Wisdom does not come overnight. [Somali]

❀ The heart of the wise man lies quiet like limpid water. [Cameroon]

❀ Only a wise person can solve a difficult problem.

❀ Knowledge without wisdom is like water in the sand. [Guinean]

❀ He, who asks questions, cannot avoid the answers. [Cameroon]

❀ A word uttered cannot be taken back.

❀ Do not show wisdom where there is wisdom. [Kenya]

❀ Wisdom breaks a taut bow. [Kenya]

❀ Other people's wisdom prevents the king from being called a fool. [Nigeria]

❀ A wise person will always find a way. [Tanzania]

❀ One, who possesses much wisdom, has it in the heart, not on the lips. [Uganda]

❀ If two wise men always agree, then there is no need for one of them. [Zambia]

❧ Even haplochromis (name of a small fish in East Africa) employs tilapia. [**East Africa**] (the senior (adult) indiscriminately doing what the junior (child) asks of him)

❧ He who learns, teaches.

❧ He, who does not know one thing, knows another. [**Kenya**]

❧ I pointed out to you the stars (the moon) and all you saw was the tip of my finger. [**Tanzania**]

❧ If you don't stand for something, you will fall for anything.

❧ If you have no teeth, do not break the clay cooking pot. [**Malawi**]

❧ If you want to know the end, look at the beginning.

❧ In the moment of crisis, the wise build bridges and the foolish build dams. [**Nigeria**]

❧ A bug grows up in dry wood, and yet comes to maturity. [**Kenya**]

❧ It is not what you are called, but what you answer to.

❧ Kachenche (a very small bird) is insignificant among strangers, but very important at home. [**Democratic Republic of Congo**]

❧ Knowledge is better than riches. [**Cameroon**]

❧ Preserve the old, but know the new.

❧ Proverbs are the palm oil with which words are eaten. [**Nigeria**]

* Seeing is different than being told.

* Wisdom is wealth.

* Tears are best dried with your own hand.

* The ears do not understand, only the mind does.

* The person who has not traveled widely thinks his or her mother is the only cook [Uganda]

* The sun will shine on those who stand before it.

* The wise continues while the fool is always beginning. [Zambia]

* The world did not make any promises.

* Two bulls cannot stay in the same kraal. [Botswana]

* Until lion have their historians, tales of the hunt shall always glorify the hunter.

* When the master of the house lacks wisdom, the doctor's work is useless. [Uganda]

* When the music changes, so does the dance.

* Wisdom is attained by learning when to hold one's tongue.

* Wisdom is like a baobab tree; no one individual can embrace it. [West African]

* Wise men may not be learned; learned men may not be wise.

WORTH

* A blind man will not thank you for a looking-glass.

* A good horse cannot be a bad color.

* A trout in the pot is better than a salmon in the sea.

* A wooden bed is better than a golden coffin.

* Far-fetched and dear-bought is good for ladies.

* Possession satisfies. [**Irish**]

* The worth of a thing is what it will bring.

* If a soup is sweet, it is money that cooks it.

Y

YOUTH

* An old banana leaf was once young and green.

* Praise the young and they will blossom.

* Young men may die, but old men must die.

* Youth lives on hope; old age on memories.

* The young cannot teach traditions to the old. [**Nigeria**]

✿ When the elderly ones in a house travel, the younger ones quickly grow in experience.

Connect with author

Readers of this book are encouraged to contact
Ms. Lewis with comments:
E-mail: *ophie2020@yahoo.com*

Connect with Ms. Lewis on
Facebook | Twitter | Instagram | LinkedIn

Get updates on upcoming books at:
www.villagetalespublishing.com
www.ophelialewis.com

All Village Tales Publishing titles, imprints and distributed lines are available at special quantity discounts for bulk purchased for sales promotions, premiums, fundraising, educational or institutional use.

For information, please visit our website
www.villagetalespublishing.com
email inquiries to
villagetalespub@gmail.com

Join our mailing list and get updates on new releases, deals, bonus content and other great books from Village Tales Publishing.

Email:
villagetalespub@gmail.com
info@villagetalespublishing.com

Like Us on Facebook
www.facebook.com/villagetalespublishing
Twitter and Instagram
@villagetalespub

Other Books by Village Tales Publishing

Available wherever books are sold.
*Children's Book

By Ophelia S. Lewis
*I'm About To
Dead Gods HM2
Heart Men (a novel)
Montserrado Stories
Liberia UnScrabbled
*Good Manner Alphabets
My Dear Liberia (Recollections)
Journeys (a Collection of Poems)
*Where in The World Is Liberia
The Dowry of Virgins (and Other Stories)

By Augustine B. Sherman
War of Morality

By Franck Olivier Houngnikpo
Message To God

By Shedrick B. Seton
The Falcon

By Augustus Y. Voahn
*Uncle Jallah Will Fix It

By Roosevelt Richards
Still I Stand

Coming Soon!
Homeless
*Little Brave Lydia
*Toby Pannoh's Good Manners for Boys and Girls

Author

Ophelia S. Lewis

The founder of Village Tales Publishing and self-published author of more than ten books, Ophelia S. Lewis is determined to make Village Tales Publishing a recognized name in the literary industry. The author of the popular heart-man novels, *Heart Men* and *Dead Gods* (HM2), Ms. Lewis has also written two collections of short stories, *The Dowry of Virgins & Other Stories* and *Montserrado Stories*; a book of essay, *My Dear Liberia*; a collection of poems, *Journeys*, and two puzzle game books, *Where In The World Is Liberia* (a children's word search book) and *Liberia Unscrabbled*. These books provide a view into Liberia society one cannot get from the headlines. Lewis has also written two children's books; *A is for Africa* and *The Good Manner Alphabets* (How to be a super polite kid).

Lewis writes full-time and lives with her family in Georgia.

Index

74, 79, 80, 86, 92, 98, 99, 102, 108, 110, 112, 114, 121, 123, 124
kindness 48, 54, 67, 113
knowledge 40, 64, 121

L

law 13, 68, 106
lawyers 46
laziness 78
liar 20, 40
Liberia 15, 26, 56, 61, 71, 72, 86, 90, 98
Libya 17, 37
lie 38, 49, 56, 62
life 12, 23, 35, 40, 44, 46, 61, 63, 79, 96, 104, 113, 116
love 24, 28, 32, 42, 49, 72, 74, 75, 77, 88, 89, 92, 96, 101, 109
loyalty 62, 74
luck 14, 74, 82, 110
lucky 74
Luo 47
lying 20, 53, 94

M

Madagascar 18
Malawi 81, 124
Mali 15
Mandingo 25
marriage 40, 75, 118
money 21, 39, 40, 46, 59, 62, 75, 77, 84, 91, 92, 97, 126
Mozambique 16

N

necessity 68, 117
Nigeria 13, 17, 49, 54, 57, 63, 69, 73, 80, 89, 107, 109, 112, 118, 122, 123, 124, 126

O

obey 34, 76
old age 63, 79, 126
old woman 26, 32, 79
opportunity 43, 80

T

Tanzania 16, 17, 32, 34, 67, 70, 79, 81, 82, 90, 98, 99, 105, 117, 119, 121, 123
teaching 114, 116
thief 20, 24, 80, 91, 114
time 15, 23, 28, 49, 50, 58, 60, 69, 73, 79, 82, 84, 85, 91, 92, 94, 95, 100, 102, 108, 114, 120, 121, 122
trials 42, 82
trouble 21, 75, 94, 114, 115
truth 21, 50, 62, 65, 92, 107, 111, 113, 119

U

Uganda 18, 36, 70, 89, 95, 96, 102, 105, 122, 123, 125

V

vengeance 18, 48

W

war 73, 86, 96, 114, 117
wealth 45, 62, 65, 87, 89, 110, 121, 125
wife 21, 36, 44, 55, 75
wisdom 14, 27, 41, 52, 90, 103, 105, 111, 118, 121, 122, 123, 125
wise man 41, 45, 46, 47, 93, 107, 111, 113, 118, 119, 123
worry 69, 95, 119
worth 23, 26, 44, 68, 82, 86, 89, 111, 121, 126
worthless 28, 85, 116
worthy 20

Z

Zambia 15, 17, 34, 47, 51, 123, 125

* 9 7 8 1 9 4 5 4 0 8 1 0 6 *